J598.5
K12b

W9-DDA-188

DETROIT PUBLIC LIBRARY

WILDER BRANCH LIBRARY
7140 E. SEVEN MILE RD.
DETROIT, MICHIGAN 48234

DATE DUE

BC-3

JUL 1998

WI

Birds up close

Birds That Don't Fly

A Bobbie Kalman Book

Crabtree Publishing Company

Birds up close
A Bobbie Kalman Book

WILDER BRANCH LIBRARY
7140 E. SEVEN MILE RD.
DETROIT, MICHIGAN 48234

AUG – 1998

For
Herbert and Phyllis

028520055

Editor-in-Chief
Bobbie Kalman

Writing team
Bobbie Kalman
Jacqueline Langille
Niki Walker

Managing editor
Lynda Hale

Series editor
Niki Walker

Text and photo research
Jacqueline Langille

Editor
Greg Nickles

Computer design
Lynda Hale
Andy Gecse (cover concept)

Production coordinator
Hannelore Sotzek

Special thanks to
Rick Andres, Anna Andres, and Big Birds of Niagara

Photographs
Frank S. Balthis: title page
Ken Cole/Valan Photos: page 8
Wolfgang Kaehler: page 25 (bottom)
The National Audubon Society Collection/PR: Brian Enting: page 28;
    Mike James: page 16; Tom McHugh: pages 5 (right), 23, 29;
    Dr. Arthur C. Twomey: cover, page 4
James P. Rowan: pages 13, 26
Tom Stack & Associates: Barbara Gerlach: page 27; Gary Milburn:
    page 20; Roy Toft: page 21; Dave Watts: page 17
Sylvia Stevens: pages 18-19
Dave Taylor: pages 5 (bottom left), 19 (top)
Tom J. Ulrich: page 5 (top left)
Jerry Whitaker: pages 12, 14 (all), 15
Art Wolfe/Art Wolfe Inc.: page 9
Other photographs by Digital Stock and Digital Vision

Illustrations
Barbara Bedell: back cover, pages 10-11, 30, 31

Consultant
Louis Bevier, Academy of Natural Sciences, Philadelphia, PA

Crabtree Publishing Company

350 Fifth Avenue	360 York Road, RR 4,	73 Lime Walk
Suite 3308	Niagara-on-the-Lake,	Headington
New York	Ontario, Canada	Oxford OX3 7AD
N.Y. 10118	L0S 1J0	United Kingdom

Copyright © **1998 CRABTREE PUBLISHING COMPANY**.
All rights reserved. No part of this publication may be
reproduced, stored in a retrieval system or be transmitted
in any form or by any means, electronic, mechanical,
photocopying, recording, or otherwise, without the prior
written permission of Crabtree Publishing Company.

Cataloging in Publication Data
Kalman, Bobbie
    Birds that don't fly

(Birds up close)
Includes index.

ISBN 0-86505-750-8 (library bound) ISBN 0-86505-764-8 (pbk.)
This book describes the physical characteristics and habits of some kinds
of flightless birds, including ostriches, emus, rheas, cassowaries, kiwis,
and penguins.

1. Ratites—Juvenile literature. [1. Ratites. 2. Birds.] I. Title. II. Series:
Kalman, Bobbie. Birds up close.

QL676.2.K346 1997   j598.5   LC 97-31454
                                                        CIP

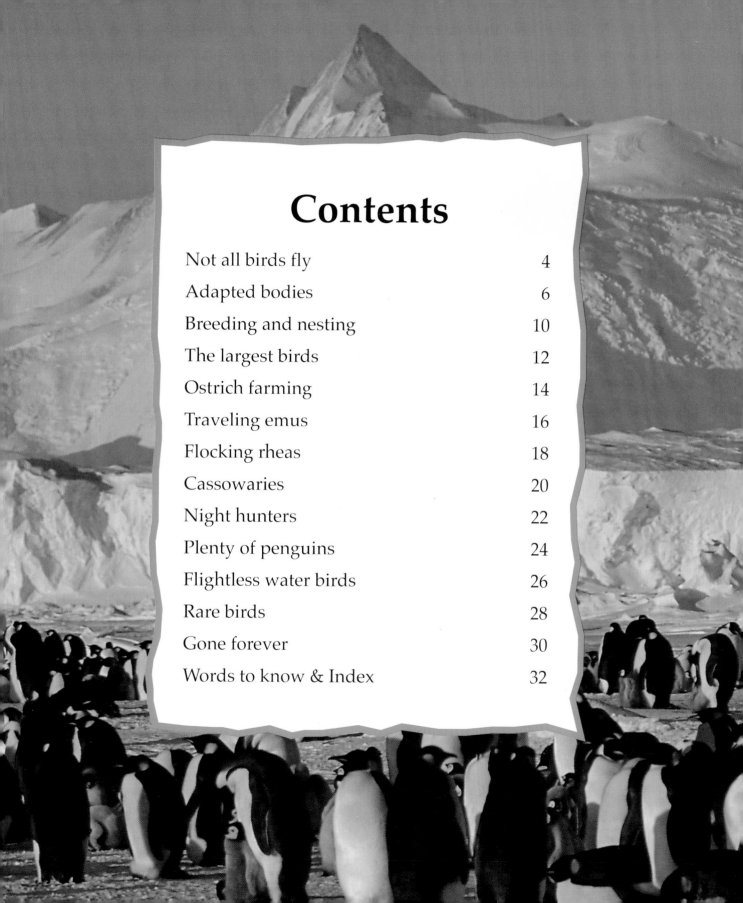

Contents

Not all birds fly

Many people think that all birds fly, but more than 20 types of birds cannot fly at all! Millions of years ago, most birds flew in order to find food and escape from **predators**. Predators are animals that hunt other animals. Some birds, however, lived in places with few or no predators. There was plenty of food on the ground or in the water. These birds did not need to fly, so they flew less and less often. Over time, they lost their ability to fly and became **flightless birds**.

(below) Some flightless water birds, such as the Campbell Island teal, became flightless in the recent past. Their duck-family "cousins" still are able to fly.

One group of flightless birds, the **ratites**, are fast runners. They run to escape danger. Ratites include cassowaries (opposite), ostriches (left), rheas (above), emus, and kiwis.

Adapted bodies

There are many differences between the bodies of birds that fly and birds that do not. They have different wings, wing muscles, legs, and feathers. Flying birds use these parts in different ways from flightless birds. All flightless bird bodies are **adapted**, or suited to the habitats in which the birds live. Compare the body of the bird below to the flightless bird shown on the next page.

Flying birds have huge muscles in their chest. They need these big, powerful wing muscles to flap their wings and lift their body into the air. Smooth, stiff feathers help them move easily through the air. Their legs are so skinny that they are not strong enough for running.

A ratite's body

This ostrich is one type of flightless bird. It is a ratite. Almost all ratites are large, heavy birds. They have strong bones to hold up the great weight of their body.

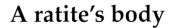

Like most flightless birds, ratites have small wing muscles. The muscles are not strong enough to lift the bird into the air.

Some ratites live in open spaces where there are no places to hide from predators. Their long neck and large eyes help them spot a predator while it is still far away.

Ratites have soft, droopy feathers. They cannot use these soft feathers to push against the air for flying.

Ratites have long, strong legs to run fast. Ostriches and cassowaries can also kick hard to defend themselves.

In zoos, people have seen cassowaries use the casque on their head as if it were a gardening tool. While searching for food, the birds use their casque to turn over fallen leaves and branches.

Helmet head

The cassowary has a body similar to other ratites, but it has a special part that they do not have. It is a hard crown called a **casque**. The casque acts as a helmet. It protects the cassowary's head from the blows of branches when the bird runs through its rainforest home. Other ratites do not need a casque. They live in areas with few trees.

Penguin bodies

Penguin bodies are designed for swimming in cold water. They have a thick layer of fat, called **blubber**, under their skin to keep them warm. Unlike flying birds, penguins have solid bones that help them dive underwater. They have stiff, paddle-like wings that push them through the water with great speed.

Penguins have large wing muscles, but they use their wings to swim rather than fly. Their legs are set far back on their body to help them swim better. Penguins steer underwater with their webbed feet.

Breeding and nesting

All birds breed to make baby birds. To breed, a female bird chooses a male bird for a partner, or **mate**. Many flying birds breed more than once each year, but they usually breed with the same partner.

Number of mates

Most flightless birds breed only once each year. Male ostriches and rheas, however, mate with three or more females in a **breeding flock**.

Laying eggs

After the birds breed, eggs grow slowly inside the female's body. When the eggs are growing, female birds eat more so that they can lay healthy eggs. The female lays one egg at a time. She must wait a day or two for the next egg to grow inside her.

Brooding the eggs

Eggs must be kept warm in order for the baby chicks to grow inside them. Many male ratites **brood**, or warm, the eggs until they hatch. Each type of flightless bird broods for a different amount of time. For example, some small penguins brood their eggs for 33 days. Emu chicks do not hatch for 56 days.

*Some penguins lay their egg on the ground. Male emperor penguins hold their egg on their feet, under a flap of skin called a **brood pouch**.*

Kiwis dig a burrow in the ground or under a log. They line this nest with grass and leaves. The female lays one white egg in the nest. Once in a while, a female kiwi lays two eggs.

Emus make a
large, flat bed of
grasses, leaves, or
twigs for a nest. Their
nest is hidden in the bushes.
One female lays between seven and
fifteen dark green eggs in the nest.

With his feet, a male ostrich scrapes a large,
shallow hole in the ground. Several females each
lay ten to twelve yellowish white eggs in this nest.
Some ostrich nests can have up to 60 eggs in them!

Cassowaries use a shallow pile of
leaves on the forest floor for a nest.
One female lays from three to
eight dark green eggs in the nest.

Rheas scrape a
large, shallow
hole in the ground
and line it with dry
grass and leaves.
Several females each lay from
eleven to eighteen yellow eggs,
until about 50 eggs are in this nest.

The largest birds

The ostrich is the tallest and heaviest bird in the world. Instead of flying, ostriches run quickly. They have only two toes, unlike other birds, which have four. Their two large toes are very strong and help ostriches run up to 40 miles (64 km) per hour. Ostriches run faster than any other two-legged animal.

For thousands of years, people have tamed ostriches to use their strength and speed. About 2000 years ago, Egyptians trained ostriches to pull carts. In ancient Rome, teams of ostriches pulled chariots in races. People still race ostriches in Africa. A jockey rides on the bird's back in the same way a person rides a horse.

Ostriches stand and run mainly on their big toe. The small second toe helps them keep their balance. They have a long, sharp toenail on the big toe of each foot. They use these toenails as weapons against their enemies.

More about ostriches

Number of species: One
Height: Up to 8 feet (2.5 m)
Weight: Up to 350 pounds (160 kg)
Habitat: Open areas, called **savannahs**, in
Africa (including deserts and grasslands)
Food: Leaves, fruit, seeds, plant shoots,
insects, lizards, and small animals
Predators: Lions, leopards, and cheetahs

Ostrich farming

At one time, people hunted ostriches for their meat, eggs, skin, and feathers. Today, the birds are raised on farms around the world. Ostrich farmers spend most of their time caring for the eggs. The eggs are important because the ostrich chicks that hatch from them grow into valuable adult birds. Adult ostriches are sold for meat, or they are used to lay more eggs.

Warming the eggs

Female ostriches can lay up to 100 eggs in a year! They lay an egg every two days. The eggs are not brooded. They are kept warm in a machine called an **incubator**. The eggs are incubated for 42 days.

Hatching chicks

It takes a couple days for the chicks to break through their shell. The chicks are wet when they finally hatch. After a few hours, their downy feathers dry off and they begin to walk.

(top) Ostrich eggs are the largest bird eggs in the world. An extra-large chicken egg looks tiny next to an ostrich egg.

(center) Farmers take the eggs from the mother birds so that they will lay more. The eggs are put in an incubator until the chicks hatch.

(bottom) Two days after hatching, an ostrich chick can run around the pen. In one week, it can find food for itself.

Nanny goats

On an ostrich farm, the chicks are kept apart from the adults. A female parent stops laying eggs if chicks are nearby. Chicks cannot stay with non-laying birds, either, because those adults have no interest in parenting. Sometimes goats act as nannies for the ostrich chicks. Goats are quiet and keep the chicks from getting upset.

Ostrich farmers keep large adults and small chicks in separate areas. The chicks crowd together for protection when someone comes into their pen.

15

Traveling emus

Emus are the world's second-largest birds. They are **nomadic**, which means they do not stay in one spot. Emus travel from place to place to find food and water. Long, thick brown feathers help them blend into tall grasses, bushes, and short trees.

Water, water

In their dry grassland home, emus need a lot of water to survive. They must drink water every day. They also need to eat fresh grass, which only grows where it rains. Emus follow the rainy seasons to find food. They are able to spend long periods in areas with sheep and cattle ranches because they can drink from the watering holes of these farm animals.

The Great Emu War

In the 1930s, emus were eating their way through many fields of grain. Australia started The Great Emu War in 1932 to get rid of the pesky birds. Only a few emus were killed, however. Today, Australia has set aside land where emus can live peacefully.

The father emu helps his chicks find the right food and fresh water.

More about emus

Number of species: One
Height: 5 - 6 feet (1.5 - 1.8 m)
Weight: 66 - 99 pounds (30 - 45 kg)
Habitat: Grasslands and scrublands in the Australian **outback**, or wilderness
Food: Grasses, grains, flowers, fruits, caterpillars, and grasshoppers
Predators: Humans and dingoes (Australian wild dogs)

(right) Parents protect their chicks from predators such as foxes, dingoes, and eagles. Emu chicks are almost never left alone.

Flocking rheas

Rheas are the third-largest ratites. They live in groups, or **flocks**, of up to 50 birds. Staying in a flock helps protect them from predators. Bush deer and cattle often graze near flocks of rheas because the birds have good hearing and eyesight. They quickly spot predators and act as watchdogs for the other grazing animals.

Each year, a male rhea mates with up to eight females. To attract females, the male puts on a **courting display** by dancing and making a special call. To begin his dance, he fluffs up his feathers. Then he swings his neck and head from side to side and runs around calling out in a deep voice. His call sounds like "NAN-DU."

More about rheas

Species: Common rhea and Darwin's rhea
Height: Common rheas 5 feet (1.5 m);
  Darwin's rheas 3 feet (0.9 m)
Weight: Common rheas up to 55 pounds (25 kg);
  Darwin's rheas up to 44 pounds (20 kg)
Habitat: Open grasslands with bushes in South America
Food: Grasses, leaves, seeds, lizards, snails, and worms
Predators: Humans and, very rarely, jaguars; hawks and
  eagles sometimes catch rhea chicks

(below) Rhea chicks eat mostly insects for the first few weeks, but they soon begin eating more plants. In only five months, they are as big as adults.

Cassowaries

*Cassowaries call to each other to attract a mate. Their call is deep and loud. When the birds make this noise, people say they are **booming**. People rarely see cassowaries, but they often hear the birds booming in the jungle.*

?More about cassowaries

Species: Double-wattled cassowary, single-wattled cassowary, and Bennett's or dwarf cassowary
Height: 3 - 6 feet (1 - 1.8 m)
Weight: Up to 187 pounds (85 kg)
Habitat: Wet, northern jungles in Australia and rainforests in Papua New Guinea
Food: Fruit, berries, seeds, and insects
Predators: Humans

Scientists know very little about cassowaries because these birds are shy. Cassowaries are **solitary**, which means they usually live alone. When two cassowaries that are not mates meet, they usually fight until one is injured and runs away.

Powerful legs

Cassowaries have such strong legs that they can run up to 30 miles (48 km) per hour. They also defend themselves with their strong legs and feet. They jump feet-first at an enemy, kicking and slashing it with their claws. The inner toe has a long, sharp claw that can kill large animals.

Fallen fruit

Cassowaries cannot climb trees to reach the fruit growing on them. They must wait for the fruit to get so ripe that it falls off the tree. Different types of trees have ripe fruit at different times of the year. The jungles in which cassowaries live must have many different trees in order for the birds to have food year-round. Unfortunately, people have cut down many of the trees that provide cassowaries with food.

Egg facts

- Kiwis usually lay one chalky white egg. Sometimes a kiwi lays two eggs.
- A kiwi egg often weighs one-fifth of the female's total body weight. Sometimes a five-pound (2.3 kg) kiwi lays a one-pound (0.45 kg) egg.
- Compared to the size of their body, kiwis lay the largest eggs in the world!
- Kiwis brood their egg up to 84 days before it hatches.
- The brooding time of the kiwi egg is the longest of any bird.

?More about kiwis

Species: Brown kiwi, great spotted kiwi, and little spotted kiwi

Height: 10 - 22 inches (25 - 55 cm)

Weight: 4 - 7 pounds (1.8 - 3 kg)

Habitat: Forests in New Zealand

Food: Earthworms, spiders, insects, seeds, and berries

Predators: Stoats, weasels, opossums, dogs, and cats (all brought to New Zealand by humans!)

Night hunters

Kiwis, the national symbol of New Zealand, are the smallest ratites. Few people see them in the wild because these birds are **nocturnal**. They are active only at night. During the day, they hide in burrows or under thick bushes.

Strong sniffers

Unlike other birds, kiwis have an excellent sense of smell. They must use smell instead of sight to find their food because they hunt only at night. Kiwis are the only birds that have their nostrils at the tip of their beak. They shove their long, curved beak into the damp soil to sniff for food. They can smell the worms and insects that live underground.

Little legs

Kiwis have short legs. To walk or run, they put one foot directly in front of the other. Try running with one foot right in front of the other. It is difficult for us to do, but not for kiwis!

Kiwis live in damp forests or pine-tree farms. They dig in the soil under fallen leaves to find the earthworms they like to eat.

Plenty of penguins

The penguin family is the largest group of flightless birds. All penguins live in the southern oceans of the world. They spend most of their life in cold water. Penguins are so well adapted for swimming that they have difficulty moving on land. Most penguins can only waddle awkwardly. Some hop from place to place instead of waddling. Others slide on their belly.

Camouflage

A penguin's black and white coloring acts as **camouflage**. Camouflage is the colors or markings on an animal that help it blend into its surroundings. Predators and prey have a hard time spotting penguins in the water. From above, their black backs blend in with the dark water below. From below, their white bellies blend in with the bright sky above.

*All penguins live in the southern half of the earth, which is below the **equator**. On maps, the line drawn across the middle of the earth is called the equator.*

More about penguins

Species: 17 different types
Height: 12 inches - 3.5 feet (30 - 100 cm)
Weight: 2 - 65 pounds (1 - 29 kg)
Habitat: Southern oceans (some come ashore every night to sleep, and others come ashore only to breed, nest, and raise young)
Food: Krill, small fish, squid, crustaceans
Predators: Leopard seals, sea lions, fur seals, orcas, and sharks; seabirds eat penguin chicks and eggs

(left) Some penguins live in warm areas. These black-footed penguins live on the coast of South Africa.

*(below) Emperor penguins push themselves on their bellies over ice and snow. This way of traveling is called **tobogganing**.*

Flightless water birds

The Galapagos flightless cormorant has ragged wing feathers that are useless for flying. After swimming, the bird's wings are soaked with water. The cormorant above is stretching out its wings to dry them in the sun.

Some flightless birds have found perfect homes in the ocean, near rocky coasts and tiny islands. Few people or other predators live there, so the birds are safe. They catch all the food they need in the water. The birds find a place to live on land only when they need to lay eggs and raise chicks.

The flightless cormorant

More than 30 types of cormorants are found all over the world. There is only one type that does not fly. The flightless cormorant lives on the Galapagos Islands, off the coast of Ecuador in South America. Its small wings are perfect for swimming and diving.

Steamer ducks

Four types of steamer ducks live on the coasts of South America. Three types are flightless. They eat crabs, mussels, and small marine animals. They can swim very quickly by paddling with their webbed feet and "rowing" over the water with their wings.

A steamer duck can flap its wings very quickly, but it will never fly. Its wing muscles are not strong enough for flying.

Rare birds

Takahes live in grassy mountain valleys where they hide from predators. They hide so well that people once thought they were extinct. A few takahes were found in 1948. People are trying to raise takahe chicks to increase the bird's numbers in the wild. The chick is on the right in the picture above.

Some flightless birds, such as kakapos and takahes, are very rare. Only a few of them are alive today. Kakapos and takahes live in New Zealand. When people moved to New Zealand, they brought animals such as cats, dogs, and stoats with them. These new predators killed almost all the takahes and kakapos.

Beautiful and shy

Takahes are shy birds with bright blue and green feathers. They are part of a group of birds called rails. Only about 200 takahes have been found alive today.

Kakapo

Kakapos are the largest parrots in the world. They are also called "night parrots" because they come out after dark. Scientists have found only about 50 kakapos living today.

Protecting these rare birds

Sanctuaries are safe places in which animals can live. Kakapo and takahe sanctuaries have been set up on small islands where there are few predators. People also raise the chicks of these birds and return them to the wild when they become adults. This type of program, called **captive breeding**, builds up animal populations.

Kakapos such as the one below have been moved to new homes on three small, safe islands.

29

Gone forever

Many types of flightless birds now face extinction. People hunt them, and some of the birds have lost their natural homes to buildings and roads. Air and water pollution kill many birds or destroy their food. A type of flightless bird can become **extinct**, or disappear forever, before people even know it is in trouble.

Extinct birds

In the recent past, more than 20 types of flightless birds became extinct. People hunted and killed most of them. Flightless birds were easy targets because they could not fly away. Many had never seen predators before and did not know how to defend themselves. These birds were hunted until there were none left.

The moa

Moas were tall birds that had no wings. They lived in New Zealand more than 500 years ago. When the Maoris moved to the New Zealand islands, they hunted moas for their meat, feathers, and eggs. The largest moas were extinct by the 1500s.

Scientists have found many moa bones in caves in New Zealand.

The great auk

Thousands of great auks once lived in the North Atlantic Ocean. Great auks were good swimmers, but they were very slow on land. Sailors and fishermen easily caught the birds at their nesting areas. Each year fewer great auks returned to their nesting places. The last pair was killed in 1844.

great auk

dodo

The dodos

Dodos are the most famous extinct birds. They lived on a small group of islands called the Mascarene Islands. They were slow, awkward birds that could only waddle. Dodos were easy targets for the European explorers who arrived at the Mascarenes in 1510. The explorers also brought new predators to the island—dogs, cats, pigs, and rats. The dodos and their eggs were hunted and eaten. The last dodos were gone by 1681.

Words to know

adapt To change in order to suit new surroundings

brood To sit over eggs so they will hatch; also to sit on chicks to keep them warm

burrow A hole dug in the ground in which to live or hide

courting Performing certain actions to attract a mate during breeding season

extinct Describing a type of plant or animal that has died out

habitat The place where a plant or animal is usually found in nature

Maoris A certain group of people who live on islands in the South Pacific Ocean

mate A partner that an animal needs in order to produce babies

nomadic Describing birds or other animals that travel long distances to find food and water

predator An animal that kills and eats other animals for food

ratite A flightless bird with a flat breastbone and small wings

Index

1 2 3 4 5 6 7 8 9 0 Printed in the U.S.A. 6 5 4 3 2 1 0 9 8 7